AF425613

Illustrations by Princess Karibo

Graphics Credits:
Yellow watercolor background by Oleksandr Blishch

1st edition 2024

Paperback edition ISBN:
979-8-9877232-3-4

Solutions 4 New Mobility Education
8 The Green, STE 4000 Dover, DE
19901
323-475-1110

Acknowledgements

Many thanks to my husband Cecil and our 4 children along with the memory of my little cousin Sammie who are the inspiration for this book series. Special thank you to Jacqueline Ramos Paz who continues her tireless efforts for safe sustainable mobility and has been a partner in bringing the series to light.

Deep gratitude to Rivian and ChargerHelp! and Founders Kameale Terry and Evette Ellis for their partnership in helping this EV story come to life. As always many thanks to my personal board of directors for encouraging my dreams Marielaina LaRosa, Latonia Early, Jacqueline Josiah and Kimberly Green.

Happy reading and safe travels!

Sammie's sweet smile and spirit is a reminder
that we want every child to live in a world
where safe mobility is possible for all.

Sammie and Sally
Go On An EV Adventure

How many can you

1. seat belt
2. electric vehicles (EV)
3. EV truck
4. EV school bus
5. booster seats
6. EV charger
7. charging station
8. GPS

mobility items spot?

9. battery
10. field technician
11. safety
12. helmets
13. bikes
14. scooters
15. remote control
16. drone
17. robot

"Mom and Dad, where are we going today?" Sammie asks.

He looks out the car window while buckled in with his <u>seatbelt</u>.

Dad smiles, "Mom and I talked – it's about time we get a new car before our family camping trip. So we're testing out some new <u>electric vehicles</u> or '<u>EVs</u>' today."

As the family walks into the EV experience space, Sally checks out the trucks, "Whoa, what even makes them electric?"

3

Mom turns to the kids,
"Well, our old car is powered by the
gas we pump at the gas station. But
our new **EV truck** will have a
battery that we can charge."

She continues, "**Electric vehicles**
plug in to get powered instead of
adding gas. Now we'll travel without
fumes that are bad to breathe, and it
is better for the environment."

Dad grins, "Are you all ready to
test one out?"

After a test drive, Mom and Dad
chat with the EV expert to learn
how to buy their <u>EV truck</u> online.

Sammie and Sally join the kids in
the play area.

In no time, Mom and Dad call out
to Sammie and Sally to head
home.

Sammie asks, "Aww, when can I
hang out with my new friends
again?"

Mom winks, "No worries, we invited some of the other families here to join us on our camping trip."

"Yay!" Sammie and Sally cheer.

6

The next afternoon, as they hop off the <u>EV school bus</u>, Sammie says, "Guess what. I had a great day at school on the playground!"

"I can tell. Did you even learn anything today, Sammie?" Sally laughs, "Did you know you can light up a lightbulb with a lemon? There are so many ways to power up electronics."

Sammie looks back at the bus. "Well I learned that I like our new school busses!"

"There's no funny smell coming out from the back anymore, and it seems a lot cleaner," Sammie continues.

Sally nods, "I like them too. I don't have to hold my nose going on and off the bus anymore!"

8

The next morning, Sammie and Sally play with their new EV truck toys.

Soon, the doorbell rings.

9

"It's here! The real <u>EV truck</u> is here!" Sammie jumps up and runs to the window.

Sally peers out the window and exclaims, "And it's in my favorite color!"

Mom calls out, "Sammie and Sally, come outside! The technician is here to get you fitted for your new <u>booster seats</u>!"

As Sammie and Sally arrive home, they see a man holding a small box in the garage with Dad.

"What's going on, Dad?" Sally asks.

Dad smiles, "We're making sure our house is ready to power our new EV truck."

"Mr. Smith the electrician is installing the latest and greatest <u>EV charger</u> in our home."

Sammie exclaims,
"I can't wait to ride in our new truck!"

Mr. Smith turns to Dad and says, "Alright sir, your new EV charger is all good to go."
13

“Thanks Mr. Smith,” Dad replies, “Do you have any tips to take care of the **charger**?”

“Sure thing. To make sure charging works correctly, make sure to protect the **cord** and the **charger** from any type of damage,”
Mr. Smith says.

“If any of you all see anything wrong, be sure to contact me right away.”

The next day, Sammie and Sally grab their bags and pack them into the EV truck.

Sally asks, "How will we charge when we are camping if our charger is in the garage?"

Dad replies, "Great question. There is charging along the way. Plus all National Parks have charging stations so we will be covered either way."

"Thank goodness!" Sammie says.

"Being stranded in the wilderness
is not my idea of fun."

Sammie, Sally, Mom and Dad hit the road. After some time, a message comes up on the car's screen. "LOW **BATTERY**," it says.

"Oh no," said Sammie. "What will we do?"

"Not to worry Sammie," said Mom, "the car will find a **charging station** and put it into the GPS for us. Look, it says there is a rest stop 7 minutes away."

Dad pulls in to the rest stop and parks next to a charging station.

"Ok," Dad said. "Time to charge the battery so we have enough energy to make it to the campsite."

A woman wearing a hard hat and a bright neon vest brushes down another charger nearby. Sally rolls down the window, "Hi ma'am, what are you doing?"

The woman says back, "I'm Betsy, the <u>field technician</u>." Betsy points to the charger, "I just repaired this <u>EV charger</u>, and now, I'm just cleaning it a bit before heading to the next one."

Sammie says, "That's so cool – I didn't even know someone had to do that. Do you have to wear that hat every day?"

"Sure do, kid. <u>Safety</u> is my highest priority. It's my job to make sure <u>electric vehicle chargers</u> are working properly with inspections, cleaning, and regular maintenance."

Betsy continues, "It's a really important job, because we need to make sure that people can charge their vehicles right away."

As Dad plugs the charger into the car, he nods, "You can say that again!"

After driving for an hour,
Sammie, Sally, Mom, and Dad
arrive at the campsite.

Soon, another **EV truck** follows
close behind.

Sammie looks out the window
and exclaims, "I think those are
the kids from the EV space!"

"Just in time!" Mom says as she walks out of the truck, "How about you set up next to us, Mrs. Garcia?"

"Okay. We have lots of food to share too," Mrs. Garcia replies, smiling.

"If you want to, you can heat it up on our new cooktop over here, Mrs. Garcia!" Sally says, pointing at the EV truck's cooktop attachment.

With wide eyes, their new friends Maya and Juan run out of their truck. Juan shouts, "Yay! We're going to have an amazing dinner!"

Maya asks, "Do we have time for our scavenger hunt on wheels before eating?"

Mr. Garcia laughs and yells, "There's always time for fun."

The four kids cheer, put on their <u>helmets</u>, and ride away.

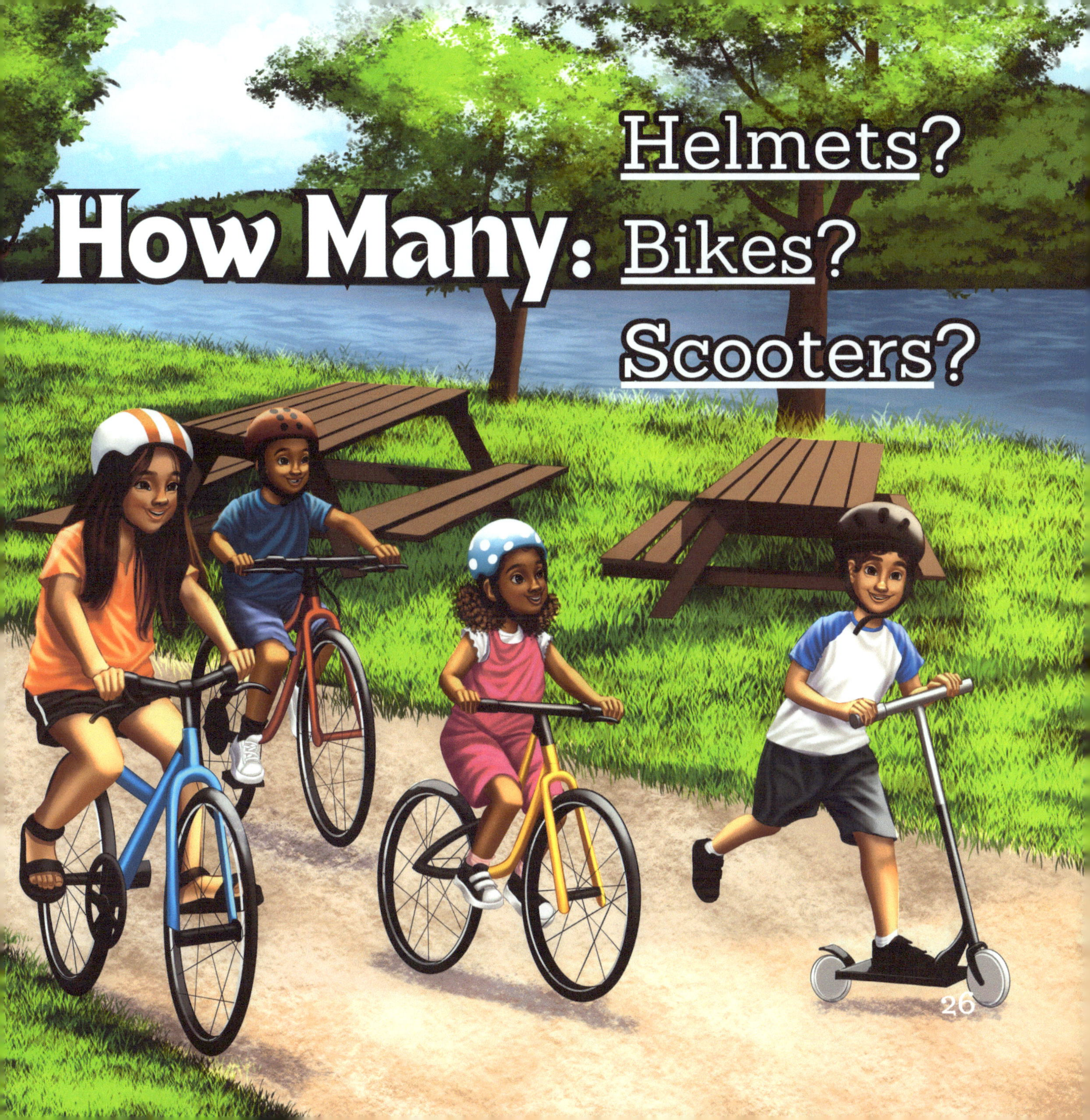

How Many: Helmets? Bikes? Scooters?
26

As the new friends ride into the campsite, they see Mrs. Garcia holding a remote control.

Sally asks, "What's that, Mrs. Garcia?"

Mrs. Garcia replies, "I work for a company that makes <u>drones</u>. Let's all take a photo with it later!" Mrs. Garcia places the <u>robot</u> on the ground and holds the remote.

"A drone is a type of <u>robot</u> that can fly and is used for lots of things like checking traffic, making deliveries, or even taking pictures."

After a successful scavenger hunt and delicious dinner, the families settle down around the campfire with s'mores.

As the fire starts to die down, Sammie whispers with a grin, "Who wants to tell spooky stories?"

Chuckling, Mrs. Garcia pulls out the small <u>drone</u>. She says, "How about we take a photo first?"

With a whir, the  **drone** starts to fly up, and Sammie exclaims, "Hold up your s'more and smile everyone!"

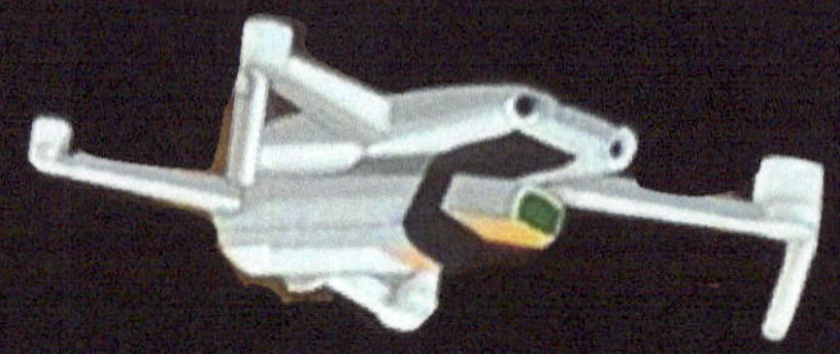

Drone safety tips:
- Make sure you fly in an area where you can see your drone at all times
- Only fly one drone at a time
- Never fly near other aircrafts or airports
- Never fly over crowds of people
- Don't fly near emergency response efforts

Where else will Sammie and Sally go?
What mobility adventure will they go on?
100% Electric
32

How many mobility items did you spot?

Selika Josiah Talbott
Author

Jacqueline Ramos
Author

Princess Karibo
Illustrator

Mobility experts Selika Josiah Talbott (founding partner of Autonomous Vehicle Consulting and former Deputy Administrator of the Motor Vehicle Commission for the State of New Jersey) and JQ Ramos Paz (transit advocate with research background in community development & transportation) with illustrator Princess Karibo (illustrator passionate about Black women representation) have created a vibrant picture book about Sammie, Sally, and their family on their fun, safe, (and often surprising) travels around the community.

Solutions 4 New Mobility Education's mission is to promote safe and equitable transportation for all, especially for kids.

www.ingramcontent.com/pod-product-compliance
Lightning Source LLC
Chambersburg PA
CBHW041607110726
48005CB00002B/316